WALLABY

THE COMPUTER DICTIONARY

written and illustrated by Mort Gerberg

A WALLABY BOOK
Published by Simon & Schuster, Inc.
New York

Grateful acknowledgment is herewith made to Edward, Timur and Kerim Friedman, and to Chris and Howard Hirschhorn, who helped research source material and translate it into English I could understand, and who read and supported this manuscript, and taught me that a computer is really my *friend*. I should also like to thank the computer that Dr. Friedman introduced me to at Stevens Tech for not biting me.

Dedicated to the thousands of people who have already overcome their resistance to and fear of computers—and to the millions who are still working on it

Published by Wallaby Books
A Division of Simon & Schuster, Inc.
Simon & Schuster Building
1230 Avenue of the Americas
New York, New York 10020

Designed by Stanley S. Drate/Folio Graphics Co., Inc.

First Wallaby Books printing May 1984

10 9 8 7 6 5 4 3 2 1

Manufactured in the United States of America

Printed and bound by Fortune Litho

ISBN: 0-671-50498-3

THE COMPUTER DICTIONARY

accessing the computer

A

absolute address The specific, physical location of a piece of data in computer storage, as distinguished from any number of places where the user has a vague hunch where it *might* be, i.e., "In There," "Down That Way," "Somewhere Over The Rainbow," or "God Only Knows."

access In everyday language, *access* is a noun, meaning an admittance. However, in computerese (and you might as well understand this here and now), words are often used in an unusual manner, so that the English language assumes characteristics usually associated with fun-house mirrors. All of which is a roundabout way to explain that computerists use *access* as a verb, as in, "I'm going to access the computer," meaning that you want to get something in or out of it. Similarly, a computerist might access a bank, a cocktail party, a girlfriend. . . .

accumulator 1. A location in a computer which temporarily stores the result of an arithmetic or logic operation. 2. A computerholic who, contrary to arithmetic and logic, buys so much that he has no location to store or operate it—even temporarily.

acronym A fundamental unit of communication (though not necessarily comprehension) among computerists. The acronym is a make-believe word formed from the first letter or letters of the words in a phrase or name. These letters may be pronounced individually (i.e., CPU for Central Processing Unit) or all together like a *real* word (i.e., BASIC for Beginner's All-Purpose Symbolic Instruction Code). Accomplished computerists can adeptly pronounce even the most complex acronyms as real words and use them in

algorithm

complete sentences with their fellows (i.e., a conversational remark such as, "VisiCalcing my personal IOCS, MICR clues the MTBF of any EBCDIC or SYSGEN, particularly on TICCIT."*) Acronyms almost always appear in capital letters to make sure they look IMPORTANT AND THAT EVERYBODY PAYS ATTENTION TO THEM.

add-on According to the data processing promotion brochures, a tantalizing, dreamlike capability to upgrade a computer's performance merely by attaching more circuitry or components, a notion of fundamental naiveté exceeded only by the belief of Ulysses' crew that the Lorelei ladies were a sweet, innocent singing group wanting only to show them a good time.

address 1. An identification, such as a name or number, for an exact location in memory which stores a unit of information not necessarily of interest to the hacker. 2. A verb meaning to greet with respect. A hacker may address his computer, "Esteemed Sir or Madam," "Revered Lord," "Blessed One," or simply, "Oh, Master." 3. An article of apparel worn by either a regular lady or by a gentleman with highly exotic sensibilities.

algorithm 1. A step-by-step procedure, essential for solving a problem, characterized by regularly repeated hand-clapping, finger-snapping, foot-tapping, and the humming of sounds like, "*Dah*-ba-dah, *dah*-ba-dah, *dah*-ba-dah-*dah*." Algorithms are created by people called *programmers*, who manifest in their work the same patience and concern for detail as do trainers of tap-dancing turtles. (See *flow chart*) 2. The first three words of a classic, popular Gershwin song.

*"The way I figure it in my own Input/Output Control System, Magnetic Ink Character Recognition helps to establish the Mean Time Between Failures of any Extended Binary Coded Decimal Interchange Code or Systems Generation, particulary in Time-Shared Interactive, Computer-Controlled Instructional Television." (Now aren't you glad you looked down here?)

array

alphanumeric A fancy term meaning the letters (from A to Z), digits (from 0 to 9), and special characters ("#$%-&!?@¢), commonly used when working with computers, as in: "The salesman said this thing was as easy to run as A-B-C or 1-2-3, that ("#$%-&!?@¢)!"

analog A method of representing information by comparing it to other, variable quantities. Thus, you might measure a log by stretching a single string of linguini alongside it and say that the log is as long as that much linguini. The novice's initial experiences with this method may cause him some discomfort in the form of imagined lumps on his body, making him feel, in computer vernacular, like a *bump analog.* (Compare *digital computer*)

ANSI 1. An acronym for American National Standards Institute (pronounce it as one word, to rhyme with "fancy"), a committee responsible for standards covering all areas of computers, except definitions. 2. How a hacker feels when he's separated from his computer for more than twelve minutes.

argument A variable within a computer experience, to which a particular value is assigned. Thus, when you or your mate first suggests that you buy a personal home computer and the other replies, "Over my dead body!" an *argument* is introduced into the function. An argument's value may be either *logical* ("If you really and truly want one, you absolutely *must* be out of your mind"), or *numerical* ("I wouldn't give two cents for your opinion!").

array 1. An ordered arrangement of computer data. 2. A shaft of light—an illumination—fervently sought by the beginner regarding his comprehension of an arrangement of data. 3. His jubilant, triumphant shout when, once in a blue moon, he finds it.

artificial intelligence A development of highly sophisticated computer systems which mimic, with rather surprising fidelity, certain functions normally associated with human intelligence, such as whining, acting cranky, refusing to cooperate, or exploding all over the place about the least little thing.

baud rate

assembly language 1. A programming language of English-like nature used by computerists when they congregate. (See *symbolic language*) 2. A choice assortment of obscenities muttered by the novice as he attempts to put together his first computer system.

---

available time The amount of time a computer system is available to a user. The more available time available to the computer user, the less available time the computer user has available for his or her career, spouse, children, lover, tennis, movies, reading, sleeping, skiing, eating, breathing. . . .

B

BASIC An acronym for Beginner's All-Purpose Symbolic Instruction Code (pronounce it like the real word), generally regarded as easier to learn than other computer languages but a tad more challenging than sixth-century colloquial Mandarin Chinese. (See *language*)

---

baud rate The manner by which knowledgeable computerists precisely express the speed of transmitting data from one device to another. For example: "NYYYYYARRRRRWWWWW!" or "ZZZZZ-ZOOOOOOOOOOOM!" or "WHOOOOOOOOOSH!" or "WHEEEEEEEH!" all express extremely *fast* baud rates. On the other hand, "ZIP," as particularly associated with the U. S. Postal Service, is commonly regarded as the slowest baud rate known to man. To correct wrong impressions, it should be noted that a *baud* itself means a unit of information transmitted per second (bps) and has nothing whatsoever to do with bawdy or lewd

binary system

behavior. This clarification should discourage dilettante hackers of both sexes whose prime reason for entering the computer field is to "make out."

binary system A rather prejudicial system of numbers that uses combinations of only *two* digits—zero and one—(as contrasted, for example, with the more liberal *decimal* system, which fully employs ten, and doesn't exclude perfectly nice numbers like 2, 3, 4, 5, 6, 7, 8, and even 9). It is believed by ultraconservative computerists to have been invented, under pressure, by the Biblical Noah, who was noted far and wide for being absolutely rotten in math, being able to add only two little bits at a time. (See *bit*)

bit 1. Generally, a teeny-weeny morsel. 2. Technically speaking, and God knows there's plenty of *that* here, a *Binary digIT* (another acronym, get it?) is either a one or a zero. Bits, when grouped together, form a number code to convey messages, not unlike a baseball catcher wiggling one digit for a fastball, two digits for a curve; or an irritated person expressing extreme displeasure by jabbing the sky with his extended second digit. 3. The whole of what a naive computer buyer goes for after being convinced by a salesman's pitch. 4. What a first-time computer user gets, which turns him into a vampire-hacker.

black box A humorous term for any computer equipment that can be operated properly by following instructions to the letter, but whose inner workings remain a dark mystery to the user, much in the same way the Neanderthal man could enjoy the warmth of the sun but was unable to express, in atomic equations, the thermonuclear phenomena which produced it.

bootstrapping 1. The process of starting up a computer by loading in just a few initial instructions, which then call other instructions, which then call in the rest of the routine. The term is based on the saying, "To pull oneself up by the bootstraps," indicating possible unconscious desires of human programmers to anthropomor-

broadcast

phize computers and let them take care of themselves. 2. Also, the process of starting up a computer by strapping on a pair of old Army boots and giving it a good, swift kick in its mainframe.

branch The instructions in a computer program that automatically switch the sequence of action along optional paths if certain conditions are satisfied, as in, "Okay, I'll get the necklace and meet you at the embassy at nine, unless the exchange rate drops 10 percent and/or the girl shows up at my hotel by eight, in which case you bring a change of clothes and I'll take Manhattan and meet you in St. Louis at eleven." If the program becomes too entangled with branches, the hacker is said to be "up a tree" or "out on a limb." Both are acceptable, though obviously not to the hacker.

breadboard An experimental model of a circuit or device temporarily tacked onto a board, giving its designer an inexpensive (for a change) opportunity to discover how unworkable his idea would be in a computer. The only people likely to spend as much time over their boards are California surfers or Russian grandmasters of chess preparing for the championship of the universe.

broadcast 1. A simultaneous transmission of information to a number of terminals. 2. A wide piece of hardened plaster encasing knuckles broken after punching transmission equipment failing to accomplish (1).

bug 1. A mistake or malfunction in a computer's program or system that resolutely resists discovery by the computerist, who nevertheless tries to locate and correct it before he a) has a small but meaningful conniption fit; b) smashes the entire system with an axe; or c) is put away for the rest of his days in a small, padded cell that has no moving parts at all. A computer expert's explanation of the origin of the term "bug" does much to dispel a widely held impression that computer people are utterly humorless. According to his account, when one of the first computers malfunc-

byte

tioned, the engineers took the whole thing apart and found a tiny, dead cockroach that had shorted out the circuits, prompting one of them to note waggishly that the reason the computer didn't work was because there was (yes!) a "bug" in the system. (See *debugging*) 2. An active verb, meaning to drive crazy, as in [shouted at the top of the lungs while waving the arms], "COMPUTERS BUG ME!"

---

bus A signal path for moving bits of data from one place to another, usually with many stops and starts and much in-between waiting time, especially when it's raining or freezing cold outside.

---

byte 1. A group of eight bits regularly ingested in one gulp by the computer. As a result, the computer may have gas and repeat; it would be better off (as Mother always said) to chew thoroughly and take smaller bytes. (See *nibble*) 2. A compelling two-word refrain ("buy it") that automatically begins echoing inside a computerholic's head whenever he passes within thirty feet of a computer store.

C

calculator 1. A device that performs arithmetic functions; usually kept in a drawer and used to pay bills once a month by ordinary people, but regarded as a life-support system and worn on the body constantly, like a pacemaker, by computerholics. 2. A jaunty farewell shouted by one computer person to another.

card reader

canned software — Ready-made computer programs that satisfy the specific needs of many users and are packaged in authoritative metal cylinders instead of in chintzy plastic bags, brown wrapping paper, or gauze.

---

card — 1. A rectangular piece of stiff paper with exact holes punched in to represent data to a computer, an inspiring example of how an accumulation of "nothing" can amount to "something." Cards may be fed by the tens of thousands into a computer so it performs one tiny operation. Another way cards may be used is to dump them out of office windows all over heroes in ticker-tape parades. 2. A practical joker whose idea of fun includes poking meaningless holes in (1) with a ball-point pen. (See *liveware*)

---

card reader — A device that reads information from cards for the future, like, for example, The Amazing Madame Ilka from Bucharest.

---

carriage return — 1. The operation that causes the cursor of a cathode ray tube to return to the left-hand margin. 2. The malfunction of the carriage of a cathode ray tube that causes its owner to curse and return it to the store. 3. What happened when Cinderella's conveyance once again became a pumpkin.

---

cathode ray tube (CRT) — 1. An electronic tube with a screen, on which information is displayed that may cause the computer user to: a) become a better informed person; b) solve a complicated problem with laughable ease; or c) kick and scream and rage like a crazy maniac. 2. The eldest son of the Tube family of Shreveport, Louisiana, who played left tackle for Texas A&M.

---

cell — 1. The location in memory for one unit of information. 2. What a brand-new computer owner contemplates doing with his unit after he's had it for one week.

---

central processing unit (CPU) — The main part of a computer system, which rigidly controls the interpretation and execution of instructions, but disclaims any responsibility for them, makes no moral judgments, offers no

chip

opinions, has no consideration for people's feelings, doesn't horse around, and won't do windows.

chain

1. A series of programs linked together so one automatically runs after another. 2. A security device by which a computer system is linked to a twelve-speed bicycle wheel. 3. A famous western movie starring Alan Ladd.

characters

1. Symbols of communication, which can express information when collectively arranged in groups. Letters and numbers, for example. Also, Miss Piggy, Kermit the Frog, Animal, and the other Muppets. 2. What your old Army unit was made up of entirely.

chip

1. A very, *very* small fleck of silicon upon which is etched an electrical circuit capable of performing more arithmetic and logical operations than all the clerks in the U. S. Civil Service. Chips come in several sizes: Micro, Infinitesimal, Itty-Bitty, Teentsie-Weentsie, and . Besides silicon, other popular chips are the potato, the chocolate, the bargaining, and the chip off the old block, particularly in a Ma and Pa computer business. 2. An adjective used by a Russian computerist to demean American-made equipment. 3. A means of transportation over water used by people from Puerto Rico.

circuit

A pathway for the flow of electrical energy. One of the most famous of these is the Borscht Circuit in the Catskill Mountains where live wires such as Sid Caesar and Danny Kaye charged around.

COBOL

An acronym for Common Business Oriented Language (pronounce as one word and rhyme with "snowball"). A high-level programming language particularly popular with giant corporations maneuvering to take over helpless companies. The use of COBOL is ordinarily confined to business offices between nine and five o'clock, as contrasted with BASIC, another programming

code

language popularly used after hours in gin joints, discos, and video-game arcades.

---

code — 1. A set of rules for converting data from one system of representation to another to make it confusing to the parties involved in the communication. For example: how many times your wife hiccups to signal a bid of three spades. Or, more to the point, the set of program instructions fed into a computer "ichwhay onay ormalnay ersonpay ouldcay eadray." 2. A headache, runny nose, and hacking cough developed as a result of sitting in front of a drafty computer.

---

command — The portion of an instruction given to a computer that specifies the operation to be performed. For example: *ADD* 100 to 400, *SEARCH* for "snails," or *GO TO* Hell. (See *operation*. Well! Go *on*! What the hell are you waiting for?!)

---

compatible software — 1. A program written for one computer that will run on a different computer without squawking about it. 2. A very friendly female programmer.

---

compile — To translate a program written in high-level language (words and phrases) into machine language (the numbers zero and one), so a computer can understand the commands and, with luck, execute them properly. Since one high-level statement normally translates into a big heap of machine language, the order to do so is colloquially, "Come! Pile!"

---

computer graphics — The part of computer technology that manufacturers boast about most. ("Nyah, nyah-ah nyah, nyah—our resolution is higher than your resolution.") (See *high resolution*)

---

computer literacy — The general knowledge and fluency with computer terms and usage with which the average grownup has only the *vaguest* passing acquaintance.

console

computer science — A field of knowledge which, according to psychiatrists, is now the leading single cause of inferiority complexes, failure to achieve orgasm, and the return to Devil worship.

console — 1. The part of a system through which the computerist theoretically can communicate with his computer. 2. What one computerist does to another whose console refuses to communicate with him.

constant — An aspect of a computer system that never changes, such as fussing with it again and again and againandagainandagain and . . .

conversational mode — The fanciful implication of "dialog" between the computer and the user. A user's entry will cause a direct response from the system, such as a logical request for elucidation; a whining protest of ignorance; a haughty stare; icy sarcasm; or a small explosion.

crash — The condition of a system that has become unusable, due to an error, malfunction, or mistake, or to the sudden, violent confluence between the CPU and a heavy, blunt instrument, such as a sledgehammer.

cursor — A darting, pulsing pointer on the video screen in the form of a square, a triangle, or the stiffly upthrust middle finger of an irate hacker, indicating either where the next piece of correct data will appear, or the exact spot where the hacker will cause his system to crash.

debugging

D

data A formalized representation of information that can be processed by a computer, consisting of numbers, letters, and symbols to describe an object, idea, fact, or concept. Some say it's "*Day*-ta," some say it's "*Dah*-ta." But then, some say, "Toe-*may*-ta," some say, "toe-*mah*-ta." Or "Poe-*tay*-ta," or "Poe-*tah*-ta." Some call the whole thing off.

data bus (pronounced *dah*-ta buss) An inquiry as to whether a particular transportation system is the desired one.

debugging The mostly illusionary process of eliminating bugs from a program or system, which might include hiring an exterminating service, swinging a dead cat over it three times at midnight, or running a special software debugger program. One of the more popular of these is named DDT (really and truly), another example of how funny computer people can be when they really want to. (See *bug*)

dedicated system A computer system which is focused on achieving a special function and works really hard on it, often staying late at the office without even asking for overtime.

descender 1. The portion of a printed letter, like "g" and "y," which drops below the line. 2. De person who drops de letter in de mailbox.

device 1. A mechanical or electrical unit with one specific purpose, the effective utilization of which is a hair's breadth beyond the user's capability. 2. How some lay people regard computers; next to booze, cigarettes, and group sex.

digital computer

digital computer — A device which processes bits of data in the form of individual digits, e.g., a hacker who counts on his fingers and toes.

digitizer — A unit that changes smooth, continuous (analog) information—like the image of a beautiful, curvy lady—into digital values of plain zeros and ones, which just goes to show how dumb computers can be.

discrete — Pertaining to separate, unconnected elements that remain aloof, mind their own business, and keep their mouths shut.

display unit — An output device for visually representing information, such as the cathode ray tube (CRT), which shows graphics, numbers, and letters; or a hacker's face (FACE), on which appear frowns, grimaces, crossed eyes, curled lips, stuck-out tongues, and beads of sweat.

disk drive — 1. A device that spins disks to access data, like a juke box playing Lawrence Welk. 2. A hacker's intense inner motivation manifested at the table where he works. 3. A street in the suburbs where many hackers live.

disk pack — A handy container of a half-dozen individual disks popularly used in a chilled state by the computerholic in conjunction with chips from a potato.

dot matrix — 1. A technique of forming letters and numbers on displays and printers from tiny dots; prolonged staring at which may cause a computerholic to become cockeyed. 2. A computerist heroine in the underground comix. 3. How an inarticulate computerholic indicates what he sleeps on in the basement, next to his equipment.

double density — 1. A technique to store twice the amount of data in a single location, like having your in-laws move in with you. 2. Very, *very* dumb [as in (1)].

double punch — The old one-two—first to the stomach, then to the chin—at the salesman who talked you into *It*.

down

down 1. The state of being inoperative, due to a malfunction in the system, as in business: "We're sorry, but the bank is unable to cash any checks today because the computer is down." Or among the self-indulgent: "Dear Aunt Miriam, Please forgive me for not writing sooner to thank you for the socks, but my computer was down." Or the *non*indulgent: "Sorry, not tonight, Honey, my computer . . . " 2. How a computerholic feels whenever his computer is inoperative.

downtime The amount of minutes, hours, days, weeks, months, years, et al., that a computer system is inoperative due to a mechanical or electrical malfunction. This is calculated by neophyte users to be approximately 47.8 times that of *up* time when, presumably, everything is honky-dory. The amount of downtime due to *human* malfunction is, of course, incalculable.

drop-dead halt A situation where the computer system, for no particular reason, stops processing in the middle of a program and cannot return to the point where it stopped, whereupon its user stands up and says to it, "Oh, my dear computer, if you were only alive, you should only drop dead!"

dumb terminal Hunnhhhh? Uhhh, better see *smart terminal.*

dump 1. To display or print the contents of a computer's internal storage, which may include memory chips, random files, bits of data, program pieces, rusty razor blades, orange peels, broken beer bottles, and sweatsocks with holes in them. 2. Where a computerholic who has put all his money into his equipment resides.

end value

E

echo check	1. A method of verifying the accuracy of the transmission of data. 2. An inaccurate one that bounces.
electronic mail	Messages transmitted through an electronic system—usually the telephone or radio—giving the public instantaneous mail service and post office executives anxiety attacks.
embedded command	1. A word processing character that gives instructions about the text without appearing in it. 2. An order issued by a computerist who is snuggled under a quilt.
end of transmission (EOT)	A signal indicating the termination of a transmission, such as a long sigh (AAHHHH), loud shout (YAYYYYYYYY!), or sudden, unexpected silence.
end value	1. A value used to compare with a count to check an operation. 2. How much you could get for your terminal.
error	Any deviation of a computed quantity from the theoretically correct value, the explanation for which is elusive. In other words, the difference between the way it *is* and the way it *should* be. A given. A fact of life, unfortunately, which you have to put up with, smash something, get an ulcer, or go crazy altogether. (Compare *bug, fault, malfunction,* and *mistake*, and while you're at it, think about whatever happened to Good Workmanship, General Competency, and Quality of Life, for example.)
escape (ESC)	There is none.
event	A processing action or occurrence that runs smoothly, completely, and accurately.

execution time

execution time 1. The sequence of a program when the actual work is done, after all that time-consuming input process. 2. The few minutes it takes to strangle the salesman who sold you your computer.

F

failure prediction 1. A technique of prevention maintenance on equipment. 2. "I *told* you so."

fan-fold paper A very long sheet of paper, sectioned in an accordian fold, used either with a printer to provide a continuous feed, or with a scissors to cut out paper dolls.

fault 1. A condition that causes a device to *not* perform as it should, e.g., a broken wire, a short, a long, a hot, a cold, a headache (the list could go on). 2. Something which human beings automatically disclaim ownership of, as in, "Well, that's not *my* fault!" This is possibly because the concept of "fault" is directly related to the concept of "guilt," and humans have enough of that already.

feedback A response by a system to an input, such as a gaseous eruption by the hacker's stomach after ingestion of three bags of potato chips, a kasha knish, and a bottle of Pepsi.

fetch To locate and load a quantity of data from storage, an action sometimes associated with the reason (we've been asked to believe all these years) that Jack and Jill went up the hill.

FIFO 1. An acronym for First-In-First-Out (pronounce as one word). An arrangement by which the first data put into storage will

floppy disk

automatically be the first retrieved, with no arguments about size places, ladies first, one data trying to sneak ahead of another, or one claiming it had an advance reservation. 2. What the Giant roared after "FEE!" and before "FUM!"

file — 1. A collection of data records, related to each other about as much as shoppers in a Macy's elevator, assembled for some vague purpose but treated as one clearly labeled unit, because neatness counts. 2. What the hacker does with his gnawed fingernails when he doesn't simply cut them off and throw them away.

firmware — Programs or data stored in a fixed way, in read-only memory (ROM), not alterable by software, nor lost when the power is turned off, like wimpware or mushware. Firmware is often built into the computer hardware, so it can't be screwed up by the liveware.

flag — An indicator of a special condition, used in software to inform a later program segment of a particular event, such as errors in prior statements. When it is all white, and waved rapidly to and fro by liveware, it indicates unconditional surrender to hardware.

floppy disk — 1. A flexible disk that provides access to stored data by being "played," like an old 45 rpm Harry James, except that it is used *in* its paper envelope *and* there's no dancing. 2. A lower back problem occurring in computerholics who sit for too long at a stretch in front of their terminals.

flow chart — A detailed diagram of symbols and interconnected lines to represent a logical sequence of errors, faults, malfunctions, and mistakes, proposed to achieve an objective in a processing system.

format — The arrangement of data into a specified layout on the ground in front of a door.

frequency — 1. The number of times a recurring signal repeats itself within a given unit of time, such as the beginner's phone call for help to his computer dealer during his first week of owning one. 2. How often (you wouldn't believe it) computer people *do* it.

glitch

G

garbage — 1. An accumulation in storage of data that is unwanted, meaningless and, in short, stinks to the high heaven. 2. A description of beautiful, shiny, brand-new computer equipment by the computerholic's unsympathetic mate, as it is being delivered into the house. 3. The results of a computer program anticipated by a nonuser.

GIGO — An acronym for Garbage In Garbage Out (pronounce as one word: *Feh*!). A saying that refers to the inability of obtaining good results with bad data. Or *bad* results with bad data. Or good results with *good* data.

glitch — An undesirable electronic interference that causes errors in a computer system and an annoying rash on the user's skin.

global search — A set of machine instructions that looks for and finds every single occurrence of any specified character, word, or phrase in a text file, completing the entire task in a matter of seconds, for no other reason than to show off.

graceful exit — When a computerist withdraws from a program, leaving his computer running, tipping his hat, making a deep bow, and blowing a kiss as he pirouettes out the door.

gulp — 1. A small group of bytes which the computer can ingest more easily than a great big greedy byte, and return to the user some form of feedback. 2. A small exclamation of surprise made by the user upon discovering that the computer feedback is actually usable.

hard copy

H

hacker — A person whose interest in and knowledge of computers is second in importance in life only to his periodical inhalation of oxygen, and who is relentlessly fervent about sharing that interest in minute detail with every visible ear, regardless of how closed it is.

halt — Who goes there? (See *drop dead*)

hard copy — The output of a machine in permanent, printed form, usually on paper, which is extremely difficult to comprehend.

hardware — 1. The various highly specialized, sophisticated, electronic, magnetic, or mechanical equipment that forms a computer system, e.g., the gizmo that looks like a combination typewriter/television set, the whozis that has hole-punched paper, the thingamajig with the whatchamacallit that you push, and all those other gimcracks. (Contrast *software, firmware, liveware,* or even *ready-to-wear,* at smart stores *everywhere.*) 2. The screwdrivers, pliers, hammers, et al., regularly used by the hacker to render his system inoperative.

head — 1. A small electromagnetic device that reads, records, and erases data and tries to make them behave nicely. 2. The part of a human's body that his mate swears has a hole in it when he announces his intention to buy a computer. (See also *read/write head*)

hello program — A "sign-on" warm-up program that is the first run in some systems, encouraging the machine to be civil with the user at

high resolution

least until he's finished his coffee. Regular use helps avoid user activation of the "good-bye program."

help 1. A precoded routine available on many systems which provides the user with information on little points that need further explanation, such as how to work computers and why even do it in the first place? 2. The most widely used term in computer communication after "Hello" and "My name is. . . ."

heuristic process A self-exploring, trial-and-error method of searching for a solution to a computer problem, closely resembling the frenzied, hit-or-miss, screaming approach most favored by beginning users. (Contrast *algorithm*)

hexadecimal Pertaining to a number system with a base of sixteen, upon which a mild but nonetheless irritating spell has been cast by a witch.

high-level language A programming language designed so users can write instructions in English-like statements while sitting on tall stools towering eighteen feet above computers. (See *assembly* and *symbolic language*)

high resolution 1. The quality of a graphics system on a video display, depending on how many image dots can be squeezed into a given area and how well they work and play with others. 2. A solemn promise of intention made when drunk, popularly at a very crowded New Year's Eve party.

horizontal scrolling Doing it lying down.

hostile environment The practice of introducing software to a system for which it was *not* designed, using special means to make the two compatible, including psychiatry, group therapy, bussing and, if all else fails, lawsuits through the ACLU.

input

I

IC
1. An acronym for Integrated Circuit (pronounce letters individually). 2. The kind of reception you get from a computer salesman when you ask for your money back.

idle characters
1. Symbols used in data communication to synchronize transmission. 2. Teenage punks hanging around a video-game arcade.

implementation
The process of installing a complete computer system: choosing inappropriate hardware, adding software hostile to its environment, and testing everything to assure the presence of bugs and the regular incidence of errors, faults, or malfunctions.

indirect address
Mail for a hacker marked "Occupant."

information
Meaningful and useful facts extracted from data which, all things considered, you'd be better off not having.

inhibiting input
1. Input that blocks production of output, because it's shy. 2. When a computerist's mate doesn't want to.

input
The introduction of raw data into a computer by a hacker who is bursting with confidence, high expectations of meaningful results, and a general feeling of well-being. (See *output*, immediately!)

instruction
A single action to be executed by the computer, which it accomplishes after double nagging and whining for triple clarification.

integrated circuit
A group of interconnected components fabricated on a tiny chip of silicon without any regard for their race, creed, or color.

interface

interactive The hypothetical ability of a system to effect immediate-response communication between a user and a machine, despite the fact that the two are usually not even on speaking terms with one another. (Remember *conversational mode*?)

interface A common physical boundary between two pieces of hardware and/or software in a system, e.g., *vere der pie iss trown.*

interlace 1. A method of addressing storage locations to reduce access time by *knot* tying them up. 2. Refers to a computerholic with a fetish for frilly underwear.

interpret To translate a higher-level language that a *person* understands and a machine *doesn't* into a lower-level language that the *machine* understands and a *person* doesn't, completing one statement at a time, very slowly, so that person and machine achieve at least the same level of mutual communication as starfish.

item A group of related characters treated as a unit—and sometimes not very nicely, either—like the crowd of designers attending a recent cocktail party for the Shah-Mata at Calvin Klein's apartment, as reported in Charlotte Curtis's society column.

J

joystick 1. A lever that can be tilted in various directions to indicate the cursor movement on a screen, affording the computerholic a degree of pleasure he might otherwise attain only through orgiastic sex or chocolate pecan pie. 2. A marijuana joint.

junk Junk is junk in any language. (A rose by any other name . . .) In this context, it refers mostly to garbled data and communication

keyboard

signals, but it is also easily applicable, particularly under non-functioning circumstances, to hardware, software, firmware, and other nowhere computerware.

justification 1. The spacing of text to produce a vertically aligned margin, unlike this one. 2. A long-winded argument, supported by convoluted statistical citations and lofty generalities, beginning with, "They say," made by a hacker explaining his addiction to a bored lawyer he's cornered at a cocktail party.

K

K 1. (Acronym. Pronounce as an entire letter, to rhyme with *Hey*!). An abbreviation for kilo, or 1000, and a loose way to describe a computer's storage capacity. Actually, one K represents 2^{10}, or 1024, which is easily remembered if you think of numbers associated with Bo Derek and Willie Mays. Therefore, an 8K computer memory can hold 8192 bytes (8 times 1024, kiddies), and a 64K memory has 65,536 bytes, which certainly is a mouthful, but then there are a lot of people walking around with I.Q.'s of 165 who don't know which end is up. 2. In a simpler life, the tenth—no, make that the *eleventh*—letter of the English alphabet.

keyboard A group of marked levers pressed manually to record characters, probably the most popular means through which a hacker can fail to communicate with his computer.

keypunch 1. A keyboard-operated device that punches holes in cards to represent data while simultaneously creating a by-product of trillions of tiny cardboard rectangles, which scientists hope will

line feed

ultimately replace solar energy, somehow. 2. A fruit-juice drink of extreme importance to computerholics.

kilobyte 1024 bytes, which if inflicted upon you by a lion, would make you dead.

kludge An odd collection of poorly matched parts that are badly fastened together to make a messy unit of something, such as the letters K, L, U, D, G, and E.

L

language A set of representations, symbols, and artificial vocabulary that allows humans to communicate (within certain emotional limitations) with computers. Among the more popular languages are BASIC, an algebraic code of modest complexity; COBOL, a terminology for business applications; FORTRAN, a high-level language for scientific computations; and VILE, a rather low-level mode of expression employed to rain torrents of invective upon a balky system.

light pen 1. An electrical device used to sketch or write directly on the CRT screen to input data or scrawl graffiti. 2. A hacker's writing implement that does *not* have a built-in combination calculator-clock-radio-razor-can-opener-toaster, and therefore weighs less than two ounces.

line feed 1. The movement, one line at a time, of paper in a printer or a cursor on a display screen. 2. What the smooth-talking salesman does to flatter a prospect. 3. What the flattered prospect swallows.

liveware

line surge 1. A sudden high-voltage condition that can damage equipment without surge protection in its comprehensive collision coverage. 2. The pushing and shoving by a mob of hackers when the computer store opens its doors for a clearance sale. 3. A type of suit worn by a hacker, usually in blue.

LISP An acronym for LISt Processing (pronounth ath one word). A litht prothething language printhipally uthed to protheth thtuff conthithting of lithts.

liveware A euphemistic reference (usually distasteful to them) to the human components of a computer system, characterized primarily by their ability to obsess. The term should not be confused with live *wire* (pronounce the two out loud), which is what some southern computerists would *like* to be known as. (Billy Joe Mason of Biloxi, for one, who could always be counted on to scotch-tape floppy disks to his forehead at weekend computer cookouts.)

log 1. A record of computer operations, listing jobs, times required, operator actions, and other pertinent data. Logs comprise the principal light reading material of computerholics, who keep piles of them (in hardcover) under their pillow, devouring them avidly, even marking and rereading titillating sections containing graphic descriptions of bizarre malfunctions, much to the despair of their neglected bedmates. 2. A basic component of a fire, into which a computerholic's mate dreams of flinging (1).

logic A science dealing with the formal principles of reason and thought which are the basis of both computer operations and all the difficulties hackers have with them.

logical decision The one of several possible courses of action which the hacker follows least frequently.

loop 1. A series of instructions that is repeated over and over, until the machine gets it right, even if it takes all night. 2. What a

machine independent

beginning user is thrown for on his first attempt. And his second. And third . . .

LPS 1. An acronym for Lines Per Second (pronounce letters individually), referring to speed of a printing device. 2. Spoken as one word, the part of a hacker's face which he bites during moments of intense frustration.

M

machine A mechanical/electrical unit that processes data, generally with somewhat fewer exhibitions of emotional trauma than a human unit doing the same job.

machine code The very first thing a hacker with a stuffed-up nose moans when he gets up in the morning to find his computer turned off.

machine independent 1. A program that is capable of running on *any* type of computer, not just under the control of one tyrannical machine, which dictates *de vay dass operation VILL BE GEMACHT!* 2. The ultimate high state of Inner Directedness sought by freedom-minded computer haters.

machine language The lowest level of language, i.e., the basic argot of a computer into which all instructions must ultimately be translated. If, for example, at a drive-in bank, you want the computer to order personalized checks printed with pictures of pet poisonous snakes, you must say, "00111100 01100100 01111011 10100110 11101011 00100101 11011010." (Note the familiar form of the verb, "10111001," properly used here in addressing a

map

servant.) Machine language is also commonly used by financial statements, regardless of their origins or areas of specialization; for example, a balance sheet from an aerodynamics company having a conversation with a profit-and-loss statement from a grain conglomerate. (In these cases, of course, the "00110101" form is preferable.)

macro instruction A code word(s) that recalls a whole set of predefined instructions designed to perform a particular operation. It is not unlike a quarterback shouting, "Red 53 Shirley Curl!" causing eleven football players in blue to automatically run around in dizzy patterns to and from specific locations, hitting eleven football players in red in order to move a leather ball six yards.

magnetic head 1. A small electronic unit used for reading and writing information on storage devices. 2. A rare physical phenomenon in which a hacker's scalp is irresistibly drawn, by a strong gravitational-like pull, to the metal part of a computer's mainframe, to which it becomes firmly stuck and can be released only by throwing a pail of hot water on it while shouting, "Gedoudahere!"

mainframe A large computer containing the central processing unit, memory, input/output, power pack, circuit boards, and (if it's *really* large) a cot for the computerholic.

malfunction A failure in the operation of the central processing unit or a peripheral device, which can clearly be blamed on a *fault*, about which the hacker should *not* feel guilty, as contrasted with a failure resulting from a *mistake*, about which he certainly *should*, if he has a shred of morality in him. (See *error, fault,* and *mistake)*

map A (out-of-date) list indicating where various elements of a program would be found if only they were put back where they belong. Available at most gasoline stations, although no longer free as they once were, they are most commonly used with a flashlight.

microprocessor

mass storage	A large capacity device, i.e., recording tape or disk, for holding huge amounts of information about certain church rituals.
megabyte	1024^2 bytes by a wild mega.
memory	The computer's storage space, usually crawling with bugs, where data is forgotten forever, misplaced temporarily, recalled occasionally, and always perceived to have been better *then* than it is *now*.
menu	A program-generated list of options on a screen from which the user can choose in order to subject himself to humiliation from a machine for several hours that he wouldn't take from a waiter for one minute.
Micro–	A prefix used to indicate one-millionth of something; for example, a microsecond is a millionth of a second (0.000001), which is really not all that slow. (See *nanosecond*)
Microcomputer	A small digital computer that incorporates a microprocessor; the very subject of our attention, a public-relations triumph of selling the world the concept that small is BIG.
Microfiche	1. A sheet of film on which images of computer output are inconveniently printed so teeny-weenily, they must be read with a microscope. 2. One you have to throw back in the lake because it's smaller than the legal size for keeping.
microminiaturization	A term implying a very small size.
microprocessor	A complete central processing unit embedded on a chip that fits on the tip of a finger. In fact, that's exactly where many scientists carry their personal microprocessors. It explains the clichéd gesture signifying the discovery of a solution, and accompanied by the shout, "Eureka!" (See illustration)
minicomputer	A fat, oversized microcomputer.

mistake

mistake A human failing that produces an unintended result, e.g., sloppy arithmetic, incorrect keypunches, or walking into a computer store "just to browse and nothing more. . . ."

---

mnemonic Refers to a technique of mnudging mnumbskulls into mnaking mnonsense mnore mnotable and mnemnorable; an easily remembered code word chosen to represent another word or phrase that is more difficult to remember, such as using "SAY" to recall—uh—to recall—mmmm—er—umm—uhhhhh??!?!

---

modem An acronym for MOdulator-DEModulator (pronounce as one word, being conscious of the unique, humming sensations produced). 1. A device that connects peripherals and changes digital signals into tones for transmission over standard communication lines, instrumental in giving computers the opportunity to do singing telegrams over the phone. 2. The first two words of a famous old minstrel song, the third and fourth words being "golden slippers. . . ."

---

module 1. A part used with others to form a larger whole. 2. An exclamation of great affection uttered by the hacker, likening any part of his system to a precious gem.

---

mouse A device that moves a cursor on a screen according to the movements of a ball rotating freely and manipulated by hand in any direction except up and down the face of a clock.

---

multiplexing The result when two or more signals simultaneously share the same line and remain independent of each other; a hacker finds this incredibly puzzling, even though he ponders it over and over and over.

number

N

nanosecond	One-billionth of a second (0.000000001). A unit of speed showing at least a little more movement than a dawdling microsecond lolling around on its amps. (See *picosecond*)
network	A series of interconnected computers communicating with each other about setting up practice schedules for a professional tennis tournament.
nibble	1. Four bits, or half a byte, which is what a slow-witted computer can comfortably ingest, so it shouldn't repeat, which can happen sometimes with a full byte, gulp, or nosh. 2. What the computer salesman hopes for when he throws out his line feed.
noise	A random signal that interferes with the flow of meaningful signals in a hacker's *own* circuit; or, the flow of *meaningful* signals in some *other* hacker's system.
nonvolatile memory	A memory that keeps its content when power is shut off and its temper when reminded of bad treatment in the past.
nosh	A little piece of herring on a cracker; maybe a half a bagel with Muenster cheese or a handful of chickpeas. (Actually, there's no such computer term; I was just kidding around.)
number	1. A symbol representing a value in a numeral system. 2. A feeling of dullness or increasing loss of sensation experienced by a normal person in a part of the body (such as the brain) after dealing with large quantities of (1) over a period of time.

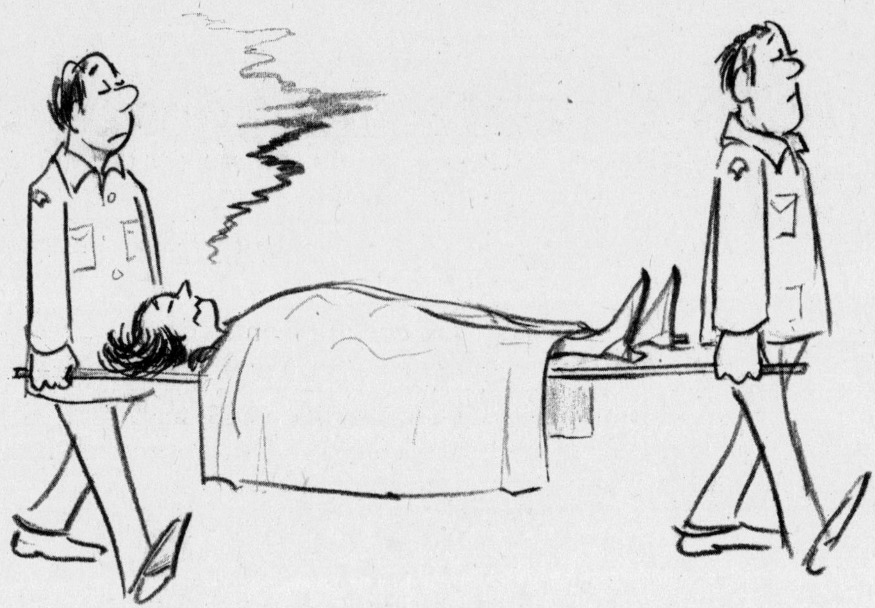

output

O

obey	A purely abstract, hypothetical concept in computers.
objective	The ends, or desired result, away from which a computer program is designed.
off line	When the operation of equipment is not under the control of the central processing unit.
on line	When the operation of equipment is not under the control of the central processing unit.
operation	An action specified by a single computer instruction, or a higher-level language statement, like a surgeon mandating a corrective, prefrontal lobotomy on a computerholic.
optical character recognition	A process by which photosensitive devices are able to identify printed graphic characters even if—as was proven conclusively at Disneyworld tests in 1982—they are disguised with horn-rimmed glasses, black mustaches, false noses, limps, and guttural Slavic accents.
output	The final result of computer processing; a sum of data, a summa dissa and a hacka on a stretcha.

plotter

P

paddle	1. A device that helps keep the cursor out of control. 2. What the beginning computer user feels he's floating up the river in a canoe without.
patch	1. A section of code inserted into a program to correct a mistake; also, a section of code in a written program that is *not* a mistake. 2. What a computerholic who spends all his money on peripherals uses to hold his clothing together.
peripheral	A device used for input/output/storage that is connected to a computer, directly; e.g., printers, card readers, and disk drives, or remotely; e.g., plastic covers for terminals, woolen paddle booties, or Plexiglas floppy disk supports, the common denominator of everything being that it costs a potful of money.
picosecond	One-trillionth of a second (0.000000000001). Hey! Now *this* is pure haste!
plotter	1. A device that produces hard copy of graphic images through an automatically controlled pen. 2. A device to use when the automatically controlled pen leaks.
portable computer	An innovation that permits a computerholic to continue hacking without interruption while going to the bathroom.
precision	The degree of exactness with which a quantity is state *d.*
printout	1. See *hard copy.* 2. A guy wearing a checkered cloth hat who talks out of a corner of his mouth, offering inside information about the running speed of a *prin.*

PROM

program 1. A sequence of extra-explicit, step-by-step instructions designed to trick the computer into performing a specific task, which the computer may agree to do when: a) you address it properly (remember the magic words, "Please" and "May I"); b) it damn well feels good and ready to; c) you call the serviceman who comes and sics The Big Master Computer on it. (See *software*) 2. An adventure of Jack Armstrong, Tom Mix, The Lone Ranger, et al., which you listened to over a radio in simpler days gone by.

---

programmer 1. A human being who designs, writes, and tests sequences of excruciatingly explicit, step-by-step instructions for a computer because he *wants* to. 2. A person who is in favor of the mother of a parent.

PROM 1. An acronym for Programmable Read Only Memory (pronounce as one word). Similar to ROM, except that a user can write into this (with the proper tools and lotsa luck). Details to follow at RAM and ROM. 2. A special school dance that you always worried you wouldn't have a date for.

---

prompt 1. A symbol generated by the computer on its terminal to inform the user, as haughtily as is possible by a machine, that more input is required for an operation. 2. A concept of rapid response to input that is inherently alien to a computer's technology.

---

protocol A set of recognized conventions governing the transfer of data between two systems or devices. For example: a CPU is not permitted to talk to a peripheral until credentials have been exchanged and they have first been properly introduced. Then the two may open lines of communication to determine which circuits will handle what, but avoiding any intimate interfacing until after cementing agreements on scrolling positions and the configurations which will trigger a final output, all of which is accompanied by an orchestrated pattern of salutes, bows, and curtsies. Then—and only then—may the two carry on.

punching position

public domain software What a program pirate calls the material he's ripping off.

pulse 1. A sudden change of short duration in the intensity of electrical voltage, sometimes resulting from the introduction into the circuit of some external input, such as the index finger of a hacker. 2. What is sought in the wrist of a hacker immediately following an occurrence described in (1).

punching position 1. A division of a card column (see *keypunch*) from which a tiny cardboard rectangle is produced. 2. A physical stance taken by a dissatisfied user, such as a crouch with fists raised, when returning to the computer store to confront his salesman.

push-down list An organization of items on which the last one added becomes the first to be retrieved, as contrasted with a push-*up* list, where the last one in is a rotten egg. (See *push-up list*)

push-up list An accounting of the consecutive number of times an out-of-shape hacker can raise and lower his stiffened body on his flexing arms.

Q

quad Refers to having four elements, the most basic of which in the physical universe are air, fire, water, and silicon chips.

query language 1. A user-friendly set of commands that allow a computerist to access information from a data base. 2. A very weird way to ask for anything; for example, (1).

read/write head

R

RAM — An acronym for Random Access Memory; twin brother of ROM, both of whom were raised by wolves.

random access memory — The computer's main storage area for programs that are immediately accessible, no matter where they're stuck, and which can be read and rewritten anytime. While RAM's mind can be changed easily, it's also a bit dotty and gets lost easily as soon as the juice goes off, so it needs to be bolstered, either by power jolts (see *refresh*) or by little memory pills, which, unfortunately, it always forgets to take. (Contrast *read-only memory*)

raster scan — A variably focused beam of electrons that illuminates triads of red, blue, and green phosphor dots on a display screen, which can create an image of Laverne. Or Shirley.

raw data — Also known as unprocessed data. A type preferred by computerholics who habitually gobble steak tartare, uncooked eggs, and live oysters.

read-only memory — A type of computer storage from which data can be only read. Unlike brother RAM, ROM doesn't forget a bit, even when the electricity is off, but is stubborn, never changes, and never learns.

read/write head — A bathroom in a data processing center whose walls are covered with graffiti written in assembly language. (See *head* (1).)

real time — 1. Computer processing that occurs simultaneously with some ongoing event in order to control its outcome. An example is an

reverse video

airline reservation system: The computer gives a ticket clerk an immediate update on what seats are still available on the plane so that he may quickly, efficiently, and cheerfully overbook the flight. 2. The only time that Real Computerists go by.

redundancy 1. The use of several devices that all perform the same function in order to increase that function's accuracy; those devices that overlap being termed, of course, repetitious. 2. The use of several devices that all perform the same function in order to increase that function's accuracy; those devices that overlap being termed, of course, repetitious. 3. Ibid. 4. Ibid.

reel 1. What a real roll of tape is really rolled on. (Rolley reeled on?) 2. A semi-vertical, side-to-side, lurching means of movement by the computerholic upon leaving his terminal after sitting in front of it for twelve consecutive hours.

refresh The continuing process of sending a signal to RAM every few milliseconds to help it remember data, tantamount to giving the old thing a shot in the head.

reverse video 1. A display technique on a screen that shows dark characters against a light background, instead of the normal other way around, the most daring innovation in computer graphics to date. 2. Sitting and watching the back of the television set for entertainment.

ROM 1. An acronym for Read-Only Memory (pronounce as a whole word). 2. An alcoholic beverage often associated with calypso music and Coca-Cola.

routine A set of sequential instructions to direct the computer to perform one specific operation, each repetition of which automatically includes a slight, varying deviation from accuracy and a different manifestation of malfunctioning.

scrolling (a little too high)

S

schematic A drawing of component connections of a circuit, not to be confused with the ink tracks made on paper by a hysterical hamster trying to find its way through a maze. Hardcore computerholics always carry yellowing, frequently folded schematics in their wallets and exchange them with other computerholics at cocktail parties, clustering together in a corner of the room near the corn chips and onion dip, nodding and murmuring, "Mmm-mmmm, oh, yeah—mmmmm, oh, yeah—mmmm. . . ."

screen type The distinction between, for example, the cathode ray tube, the liquid display, the light-emitting diode, Marilyn Monroe, Lauren Bacall, and Jane Fonda.

scrolling 1. The act of moving text vertically or horizontally on a display so that the unseen portions can be viewed on the screen, giving the user a sense—as small as it is—of at least *some* success.

semiconductor 1. A material with electrical conductivity and resistance that ranges between high and low, varying with changes in temperature around it, just like a mate. 2. An orchestra leader who only plays half-notes.

sense 1. To examine or determine with respect to a criterion. 2. That which most people still can't make out of computers.

sequence A precise, prearrangement of items or events in either ascending or descending order, occurring at the same time for both brief and lengthy duration, overlapping each other, while pushing, shoving, and carrying on.

smart terminal

serial 1. Pertaining to the sequential occurrence of two or more related activities, e.g., eating lunch after *first* eating breakfast. 2. What is eaten for breakfast.

---

sign 1. A symbol used in the arithmetical sense to describe whether a value is positive or negative, such as a thumb-to-the-nose gesture in response to the first price the wily computer salesman quotes you. 2. What you do at the bottom of each check to pay for all the peripherals the wily computer salesman sells you.

---

slave One device operating under the control of another device, i.e., a hacker sitting in front of his computer.

---

smart terminal A device that has its own microprocessor and control electronics, allowing it to function independently, move up quickly, and—if it's got guts as well as smarts—maybe even take over the whole operation. 2. In a fast repartee, the final rejoinder that tops everything that was said before, such as, "The same to you, Buddy!"

---

software 1. The programs that tell the computer which operations to perform. Computerists put their software on *over* their hardware, a procedure exactly the reverse—it is mildly interesting to note—of that followed by King Arthur's Knights of the Round Table or the Green Bay Packers. 2. A repugnant (to feminists) euphemism denoting female programmers.

---

solid state 1. Descriptive of components which control electrons in solids; for example, handcuffs, chains, and prison cells. 2. Where most of the population follows straight, conventional lifestyles (*not* California).

---

split screen 1. A display in which a program divides the screen into two separate areas for simultaneous viewing, thereby providing a new user with an opportunity to double his confusion quotient (CQ). 2. The way Buddy Hacket, doing his Chinese waiter impersonation, would say, "*sprit scleen.*"

superscript

sum A quantity which results from adding other quantities incorrectly; also spelled "some" by beginning users.

superscript A letter or digit written above a symbol (x^2) to denote a power greater than a locomotive, faster than a speeding bullet, and able to ^{leap} tall buildings in a single ^{bound}.

suppress To eliminate zeros or other insignificant characters from a computer printout, even though the hacker may find them achingly beautiful to behold, or are among those with which the hacker has formed a powerful, personal relationship.

symbolic language A pseudolanguage made up of letters, characters, and numbers, which must be translated into machine language for the computer but which is comprehensible to hackers because of its humanlike nature. Hackers often use symbolic language in front of computers when they don't want the units to know what they're talking about.

syntax 1. The grammatical rules of a programming language. 2. A government surcharge on lust, envy, greed, et al.

T

teleprinter 1. A form of typewriter used in transferring data over communication lines, which doesn't need anyone dozing in front of it, sticking chewing gum on it, or dripping coffee and liquid paper all over it. 2. Your response to your assistant's report of errors on proof sheets.

terminal

terminal 1. A device (like the television/typewriter combination) that theoretically processes the input and output of data and by means of which the computer and user enact an artful charade of communication. 2. The condition of a computerholic who sits in front of (1) twenty-four hours a day.

time sharing 1. A computer facility that serves a number of users at different locations, near or far, for different purposes, all at (apparently) the same time, using no mirrors, no wires, with nothing up the sleeve, and at no time do the fingers ever leave the hands. 2. When several programmers use the same wristwatch in the office.

touch terminal A device that the user physically interacts with by actually touching the screen, with a finger in order to choose an input, or a foot for its output.

transistor An electronic component that controls the flow of current, the invention of which caused an instant wave of despair to flow over all the manufacturers of vacuum tubes. (See *vacuum tube*)

translator 1. A program that converts incomprehensible statements in one language into correspondingly incomprehensible statements in another language. 2. A person (usually no older than fourteen), who is equally fluent in both computerese and humanspeak, such as English, therefore an essential companion if you are accidentally approached on the street by a computer salesman or if you are invited to an international computerist cookout in Silicon Valley.

truncate To cut off the least significant digits of a number for simpler and speedier handling. For example: the number 3.14159 truncates the series for *pi*, which could be carried on indefinitely but then could not be thrown so easily.

truncation error When the barber takes too much off the top.

user friendly

turnaround time A measure of systems performance based on the time it takes for a job to go from the user through the computer operation, and then back to the user with some form of program results, a shorter period, it is hoped, than waiting for Godot.

turnkey 1. A system that is complete and ready to run when it is turned over to the user, who needs to do nothing but "turn the key" in the panel lock and start using it—provided, of course, that the key is included, and that it is the correct key, and fits, and activates . . . 2. The name of a barnyard fowl, sometimes used to describe a system that doesn't run the way it is supposed to.

U

UG An acronym for User Group. (Pronounce letters individually if a member of the group, and altogether as one word—UGH!—if an outsider.)

user friendly 1. A characteristic of software and hardware systems that are supposedly easy for a user to learn to operate without much specialized knowledge or training, a representation whose truth quotient is about the same as "The check is in the mail." Actually, the phrase is literally accurate, since the user himself is *friendly.* His system, though, is *hostile.* 2. What a tough-talking street kid grudgingly admits to a group of social workers who have been kind to him.

user group People who share experiences, knowledge, and programs about a system they are all familiar with, through meetings and/or publications, such as Alcoholics Anonymous.

vendor

utility routine — A type of software that performs frequently required functions necessary to the uninterrupted, smooth-running operation of a computer system, including copying programs, reordering programs, replacing worn-out human operators . . .

V

vacuum tube — The dominant electronic element in the computer's Neanderthal days, B.T. (Before Transistors). A computer using vacuum tubes today may be likened to the Queen Elizabeth powered by sails, and the mere glimpse of one by young hot-shot hackers can propel them into uncontrollable paroxysms of irreverent laughter.

validation — The examination of data for accuracy, by checking it against a vast assortment of previously established criteria, a mind-numbing process which gobbles up huge chunks of the computerist's time, often provoking him to seek validation for his devotion to computers.

variable — 1. A quality (or symbol) in a computer program (or any other plan in life, for that matter) used to represent a value (either this, that, or the other), which can then be changed to something else, anytime, anywhere (except for Clark Kent), in the middle (or beginning or end) of the program's execution. Also spelled, *varyable.* 2. The life of a free-lance cartoonist and/or writer.

vendor — An individual or company that sells computers, computer services, and peripheral devices of every kind, often preying on

voice recognition

unsuspecting innocents, hooking them on soft stuff, then gradually pushing unspeakable, harder ware, increasing their addiction until they turn into serious users and hopeless computerholics.

vertical scrolling Scrolling while standing up.

video monitor 1. A television screen that only displays information, without a sound, the same way, day after day, having no controls or intelligence of its own but depending totally on signals from the computer. Some job, huh? 2. The kid in school responsible for making sure all the computers are turned off after class.

VisiCalc™ A popular software program that enables its user to make instant calculations in solving mathematical problems, such as paying bills, so he more quickly realizes that he's flat broke.

voice recognition The ability of a computer to accept verbal commands. The user must take care to pronounce each word slow-ly, pre-cise-ly, and dis-tinct-ly, as if requesting directions from a traffic cop in Ljubljana, remembering *not* to talk with your hands, and assuming a tone of voice that communicates authority without hauteur, warmth without weakness, and friendliness without equality. Voice recognition can work only within certain narrow parameters; addressing the computer with a high-pitched "Guess Who?" in a Swedish accent is not recommended.

volatile memory A storage area that does not retain its information content when: a) the power is turned off; b) it becomes senile; c) it is soaked in too much Jack Daniels the night before; d) it is miffed and just doesn't *want* to.

word processing

W

wafer A very thin circular slice of solid silicon that is diced into chips (cir-*cuits*) instead of being eaten wholly, as is the custom in certain religious ceremonies.

wait state A difficult period of time for a computer system, when it is not being used, due to a lack of demand, perhaps because of a falling off of interest on the part of its owner who doesn't call and who, come to think of it, may very well be out running around with another system.

word processing 1. A computer program with vast capacities for typing, editing, revising, manipulating, arranging, storing, and printing manuscripts, but no capacity at all for thinking up ideas and creating sentences. 2. What William Shakespeare, for one, did with pen and paper.

wpm An acronym for words per minute. Pronounce letters individually or together as a whole word, representing a command to flail a male secretary because his shorthand is too slow.

X

x 1. A symbol used to denote an unknown factor, such as the probability that a normal person can assimilate new, alien tech-

Y

nology about computers and live happily ever after. 2. An acronym for "ex," referring to some state or condition that was viable in the past but no longer in the present, as in, "*ex*-computer owner."

Y

Y Because as long as the human race has existed here on Earth, it has continually and courageously endeavored to boldly explore uncharted territories of Beingness and stretch the limits of its potential to more fully actualize the life experience. Next question?

Y-punch 1. The twelfth position on a punch card. 2. A position taken by pacifists in debates on violence.

Z

zap 1. An intentional program command that clears the screen, much in the same manner that Krinkons are eradicated in Space

Shnooks. 2. Unintentional program overwriting that gets the same result, sometimes accompanied by a small fire with lots of white smoke.

---

zero 1. One-half of a computer's entire vocabularly (see *machine language* again; maybe you'll get it this time). 2. To computer haters, the number of acceptable arguments in favor of computers and their people. 3. To computerholics, a number representing the total value of life without computers. 4. The number of definitions following this one.

zero